Hymn to
the Canadian Rockies

Art Aeon

Hymn to the Canadian Rockies by **Art Aeon**

ISBN 9781988038193

Publisher: AEON PRESS, Halifax, Nova Scotia, Canada
E-mail: canaeonpress@gmail.com

An old version of this book was published in 2004
under the title, *Hymn to Shining Mountains:
The Canadian Rockies* by Art Aeon.

<Revised Feb 2025>

Books of Poetry by Art Aeon

Flowing with Seasons (2003)
Hymn to Shining Mountains: The Canadian Rockies (2004)
In the Range of Light: The Yosemite (2005)
Snowflakes on Old Pines (2006)
Prayer to Sea (2007)
Echoes from Times Past (2008)
Breathing in Dao [道] (2009)
The Final Day of Socrates (2010)
Beyond the Tragedies of Oedipus and Antigone (2011)
Dù Fǔ [杜 甫] *and a Pilgrim* (2012)
The Yosemite: Images and Echoes (2013)
Revealing Dream of Vergil (2014)
Homer and Odysseus (2017)
Socrates with Xantippe on his Last Day (2019)*
Tragic Comedies of Humans (2019)*
Du Fu [杜 甫] *with his Last Pilgrim* (2019)*
Virgil's Last Dream of Aeneas and Homer (2019)*
Following Homer's Odyssey (2020)*
Human Causes of the Trojan War (2020)*
Awakening to One's Conscience (2020)*
Dante's Sublime Poem of Light (2022)*
On the Nature of Humankind (2022)*
Cosmic Drama of Nature (2022)*
Tribute to Mentors and Friends (2023)*
Pilgrimage into Classics (2024)*
Simple Songs on Life in Nature (2024)*
Inner Voice{2000-2007}: Simple Songs on Nature(2024)*

*Distributed worldwide by Amazon.com as printed books
and by Google Play Books.com as electronic books.

Art Aeon

*Hymn to
the Canadian Rockies*

For Everyone
Whoever admires at heart
the magnificent beauty of nature,
and reveres its sublime spirituality.

List of Poems

List of Poems

List of Poems

Shining Mountains

Midway on the journey of our life,
a humble pilgrim visits
the Canadian Rockies
to behold the sublime lights.

Magnificent peaks crowned
with shining glaciers,
welcome him in solemnity.

The glorious sun sets in the alpine glow.
A serene dusk pervades
the verdant valleys in peace.

The elated pilgrim prays,
inspired in awe and wonders.
The sacred spirit of lofty mountains
permeates deep in his meek soul.

A Night in High Mountains

I lodge at an alpine hut
beneath towering mountains.
How wondrous it is to rest
in the bosom of nature.

Fresh mountain air refreshes
my exhausted, aching body.
Delightful excitements
keep me awake till late at night.

Beautiful stars twinkle
in the tranquil mountain sky.
Blissful peace nestles
deep in this empty mind.

Early Dawn in Mountains

Sublime, sheer peaks loom
afloat above subtle mists
in ethereal twilights
of calm, pristine dawn.

They look rapt in deep
timeless meditation,
waiting to be awakened
in an enlightened realm.

Sketching in Word

With plain, formless words,

I strive to sketch what I see

in breath-taking bliss.

A Symphony of Mountains

A vast sea of mountains glitters
in resplendent morning sunbeams.
A pristine river sings in vital rhythms,
meandering through lush forests.

Here exults nature in solemn grandeur.
A meek man exalts her in a trance:
*"Listen to this grand symphony of mountains,
singing in spiritual lights!"*

Morning Calm in Mountains

Morning calm pervades
a pristine, clear lake.
Wildflowers relish
sparkling, fresh dews.

The splendid sun rises
above majestic peaks.
The serene lake reflects
the wonderful sight.

A wanderer pauses
by the gleaming lake,
wondering whereto
this daydream leads him.

Blessed Tranquillity

Calm before sunrise—

Sublime peaks and serene lakes

breathe in eternity.

The Valley of the Ten Peaks

The Valley of the Ten Peaks shines
in awe-inspiring sights
like solemn, mighty titans
in a divine council.

What profound matters
are they discussing
in such prophetic,
deep silence for aeons?

A graceful, limpid lake
nestled in the middle
reflects a subtle light
on their profound mystery.

Celestial Castles

The magnificent expanse
of high mountain ranges
looms mysteriously aloft
like a grand celestial castle.

Impressive clouds shroud
the hidden summits
as if they stand on guard
the sacred mystery.

Thunderstorms in Mountains

Dark clouds shroud sheer peaks.

Thunderstorms strike in splendours.

A man watches in awe.

Alpine Meadows

Exotic flowers dance
in lush alpine meadows.

Handsome mountain goats roam
freely on steep rocky cliffs.

A stout eagle floats aloft,
motionless in mid-air.

A meek pilgrim bows
to wonders of nature.

Meditation

A sublime mountain

muses deeply on a pristine lake

in a breath-taking trance.

Prayer in Bliss

Delicate mists caress
immense, pristine glaciers.
Lush, green forests bedeck
a calm emerald lake.

The glorious sun sets
between towering peaks.
A noble eagle glides
in the limpid blue sky.

Tranquillity deepens
in the peaceful valleys.
A meek pilgrim prays
with heartfelt thanks in bliss.

Sentinel Pass

Above the scenic *Valley of the Ten Peaks*
through lush forests of larches
I crawl up steep *Sentinel Pass*.

Spires of stark rocks soar into the sky
with austere expressions,
exulting in solemn grandeur.

Dreamlike Mountains

Twilights of an early dawn
shimmer on high mountains.
Their subtle silhouettes loom
like mighty titans sound asleep.

How mysterious they look.
What awe they inspire.

Some time ago, they lay deep
beneath the primordial sea.
Now, they seem to soar up high
to reach the celestial vault.

Am I awake amid these dreamlike mountains?
Or do I imagine them in an ephemeral dream?

Temple Mountain

At sunrise, I start to climb up
a majestic mountain.
Its summit, clad with glaciers,
looks like a hallowed temple.

Suddenly, dark clouds clash
on stark, sheer cliffs.
Icy hails block perilous trails.
Thrilled in awe, I retreat.

By a singing stream, I pause
to catch my breath and quench my thirst.
In sparkling icy water,
I wash my dusty body
and cleanse my rusty mind.

Soon, the alpine storm stops.
Bright sunbeams warm my heart.
Here, I feel a vital breath
of the sublime mountains,
gently permeating my soul.

Banff Hot Springs

How good it is to bathe
in a balmy hot-spring pool
atop a scenic mountain.

The soothing water possesses
a magic power that heals
the mind as well as the body.

The refreshed wayfarer
bows to gracious nature,
glowing in a calm sunset.

{18}

Mountains at Dusk

Dusk shrouds high mountains.

Sheer mists waft on serene lakes.

They become sheer dreams.

Mountains at Sunrise

The rising sun suffuses
magnificent lofty peaks.
Exquisite glaciers glow
ablaze with ardent passions.

A serene lake reflects
this breathtaking scenery.
A humble soul breathes in
the sacred spirit in awe.

On Moraine Lake

Beneath lofty peaks soaring up the sky,
my canoe glides on limpid water.
A lucent reflection of jagged, tall spires
suffuses the calm lake in wondrous splendours.

A serene sunset imbues
stark rocks, lush forests, and pristine glaciers
with mystic, spiritual glows.

The ethereal range of subtle light and shade
reflects on this lake in eternal peace.

The Icefields Parkways

The Icefields Parkways weaves
through endless mountain ranges.
Countless majestic peaks
enchant my astounded vision.

Pristine glaciers prevail
since time immemorial.
Resplendent lakes repose
in an unearthly peace.

Ever-changing clouds
hover over soaring peaks.
The vast panorama unfolds
in a cosmic drama.

How much further should I
pursue these awesome paths
to reach the very heart
of these shining mountains?

Creeping on Cliffs

Sheer peaks soar up high.

Vast glaciers feed pristine lakes.

A man creeps on cliffs.

Morning Prayer

Subtle mists sweep dreamy peaks
in ethereal calm at sunrise.
Sacred, vital spirit hovers over
these hallowed lofty mountains.

A graceful lake reflects
subtle images of mysterious realms.
An elated pilgrim prays
for inner awakening.

A Glimpse of the Columbia Icefields

From the summit of *Parker Ridge*
I behold the immense expanse
of the *Columbia Icefields,*
hidden aloft on top of this world.

I gaze at *Mount Columbia* from afar:
Amid the vast sea of ageless ice,
the sacred white mountain looks
soaring up to reach the high heavens
like a spirit embodied in light.

{25}

Crawling on Glacier

On a vast glacier

a speck of paltry clod crawls,

trembling in awe.

On Athabasca Glacier

The immense frozen sea of ice
looms in awesome grandeur.
Solid rivers of glaciers flow
in prophetic, deep silence.

Ever-changing clouds
wander freely in the sky.
Sheer, misty vapours arise
like cold flames of strange fires.

Vital breaths hover over
this ethereal, mystic realm.
Exquisite forms emerge
from ageless, pristine ice.

The pallid sun sets
on the frozen horizon.
An elated man bows
in awe and heartfelt humility.

Bow Lake

Wandering through desolate icefields,
I come across a gracious, peaceful lake.

Limpid, emerald water glitters
at calm sunset on long journeys to seas
through lively singing streams.

Enchanting flowers
bloom along the lakeshores.
How gently they soothe my heart!

A subtle mixture
of delight and despair
overwhelms the wanderer's
tender yearning heart.

{28}

On Trails

Steep trails spiral up.

A climber clings to the cliff's edges

in quick thunderstorms.

Peyto Lake

Lush, green meadows meet
white, pristine glaciers,
nestled at the heart
of a lofty mountain.

Wildflowers embroider
the neat, alpine highlands
in vivid, resplendent
patterns of primary hues.

A wanderer pauses by
a shy, tender flower.
She whispers to him:
"Welcome to our home."

Athabasca Falls

The gush of snow-melt water
rushes through deep canyons.
Colourful rainbows waft
over resplendent sprays.

Soft water carves adamant rocks
into exquisite sculptures.
Exotic mosses flourish,
creeping on steep, rocky cliffs.

Thunderous roars reverberate
through extraordinary, deep chasms.
They turn into prophetic songs
for an awe-inspired soul.

Here sings Mother Nature
in her noble grandeur.
Here, a meek child listens
to her deep, wise voice.

Sunwapta Falls

Vibrant, sparkling streams

sing and dance over stark, hard rocks

with enthralling zests.

Medicine Lake

The gorgeous sunset
suffuses a serene lake.
A strange little bird
sings in enchanting tunes.

A wayfarer wades freely
in the fresh, clear water
to purge his mind
from vain, worldly worries.

This enthralling lake soothes
the lonesome wanderer
as a loving mother
lulls her dear little child.

View from Spirit Island

Sacred lofty mountains
loom in solemn grandeur,
looking into the lake
like gods rapt in deep thought.

How gently they converse
with the ethereal lake,
reflecting on the mystic spirit
in ineffable eloquence.

Bow River

Quick, vibrant currents
of glacial water sing
in exuberant rhythms
of sheer vitality.

How long has this river
kept on running to the sea
from its sacred fountains,
hidden in high mountains?

A humble wayfarer
pauses by the scenic bank,
admiring lively flows
of this thundering river—
utterly forgetting of himself
who flows fast in the mystic river of time.

Lake Louise

Lofty peaks appear and disappear
in freely drifting clouds.
Precipitous feet of glaciers
nourish the pristine lake.

Fragrances of exotic flowers
permeate in fresh morning breezes.
A lovely tune of a strange bird
echoes in the peaceful lakeshore.

The lake reflects the sublime view,
gleaming like a mystic mirror.
A breath of eternity pervades
the inner realm of a meek soul.

Night Prayer by Lake Louise

Dusk deepens in the mountains.
The tranquil lake reposes
in heavenly peace.
Starlight suffuses the calm water.

A pilgrim sits by the lake,
praying in solitude.

May he see someday
an awakening light,
shining from an inner lake,
hidden deep in his soul.

Twin-Falls in Yoho National Park

At a splendid sunrise,

Twin-Falls thunders in grandeur

afloat on misty rainbows.

Takakkaw Fall at Sunset

The glorious sun sets.

Tall *Takakkaw Fall* glows ablaze,

as if rising to the heavens.

Angel Glacier on Mount Edith Cavell

A noble mountain
smiles in the calm sunset.
It embraces so tenderly
a graceful glacier,
clinging to its gentle bosom.

How sacred they look—
Mother and child confide
blessed love beyond words
in mysterious rhythms
of eloquent silence.

Campfires in High Mountains

Hikers old and young meet
around campfires,
sharing joys and woes
in the journey of our life.

The strangers become friends,
as if they had been dear old comrades
in the struggles for existence.

Twinkling stars seem to come down
from the mysterious night sky
to overhear what we talk about.

Blessing on the High

Lofty *Angel Glacier*

alights on the peak, blessing us

with heavenly grace.

Moonlit Glaciers

The bright full moon rises
above lofty peaks. Vast glaciers gleam
in breath-taking still.

A man strives to draw
the sublime scene on his soul
rapt in awe and bliss.

{43}

Sanctuary in Jasper National Park

A young fawn nuzzles

her mother doe: how lovely

they talk without words!

Decent from Athabasca Glacier

Sheer crevasses block passes.
I pause to admire
austere grandeur in deep still.

How lonesome to be
forlorn in the vast sea of ice—
Yet, it is so wondrous to be here!

The pallid sun sets.
Pensive steps move on the vast ice
in deep solitude.

{45}

Climbing Up

The more I struggle

to climb up, the higher rises

the mystic summit.

The Valley of the Ten Peaks at Sunrise

Fresh sunrise imbues
lofty peaks with glorious lights.
It sets glaciers ablaze.

The calm, vivid lake
paints the ethereal scenery
with fervid passions.

A meek man strives
how to breathe in such sublime
splendours in pure bliss.

{47}

Maligne Canyon

A stark, stout rock splits
huge, fast gushes of water.
Thundering torrents splash
in majestic splendours.
These vibrant movements infuse
vital spirit deep into my soul.

All things are flowing
in the river of time.
Yet, my brief sojourn here
seems to be timeless.

May the sacred spirit
of these sublime mountains
inspire me to sing of nature
deep from my meek heart.

Musing while Moving

I toil to climb up.
Amid this journey of our life
I look for the light.

The summit I reach.
How wondrous it is to attain
the goal of striving.

The divine panorama
overwhelms my mortal vision.
In bliss, I exult.

Descent at sunset—
I muse about how to pursue
an inner journey.

Home for Spirit

My first brief pilgrimage
to the *Shining Mountains*
fleets away like a daydream.
Tomorrow, must I leave here
to resume my worldly toils.

In a pensive mood,
I move my heavy solitary steps down,
pondering where in this world
I should find a home for my spirit.

Reflection on Oneself

Bidding a heartfelt farewell
to these spiritual mountains,
I catch my train at a pale sunset.

It prowls through hard passes:
Spiralling up steep crags and
creeping down along perilous gorges.

Countless pitch-dark tunnels seem
endlessly long to pass through.
Pitiful panting of the striving iron-horse
resounds with the throbbing heartbeat
of its pensive passenger.

It rains in the sad evening.
Dusk veils sheer landscapes,
fleeting by the dark windows:
It reflects a pair of earnest eyes,
looking deep into my soul.

The book-cover photograph of *The Valley of Ten Peaks* Banff National Park of Canada was taken by the author.